- Live each day as your life
- Its not what happens it is how you h

Humility and responsibility are the cornerstones of my progress.

First published September, 1989.

ISBN: 0-89486-616-8

Printed in the United States of America.

Designer: Maria Mazzara
Illustrator: Susan Kirkham

Editor's Note:

Hazelden Educational Materials offers a variety of information on chemical dependency and related areas. Our publications do not necessarily represent Hazelden or its programs, nor do they officially speak for any Twelve Step organization.

The quotations contained on each of the pages of this journal have been compiled from the extensive spoken tradition of the Twelve Step programs. Hazelden recognizes the quotations as belonging to the public domain and claims no ownership of any particular saying.

CORNERSTONES

A Journal with Inspiration from
the Twelve Step Spoken Tradition

 HAZELDEN®

For serenity, three ingredients must be in balance; mind, body, and spirit.

Progress not perfection.

Learn to listen; listen to learn.

Time is God's way of preventing everything
from happening all at once.

I'm in charge of the effort, not the result.

Action conquers fear.

If I keep doing what I'm doing, I'll keep getting what I'm getting.

When one door closes another door opens.

I am only an expert on my own opinion.

Prayer is talking to God; meditation is listening to God talk to me.

Act as if.

Don't sweat the small stuff—it's all small stuff.

Bring the body—the mind will follow.

In recovery, I don't think less of myself;
I just think of myself less.

Live to love; love to let live.

This is a simple program for complicated people.

Pain is normal, suffering is optional.

When I don't feel close to God, who moved?

non-judgemental: Art activity - passing Art project to person next to us, we would never look at a Childs art & say that it's hideous. Now same goes for your neighbor. So I've just shown you how to create w/o judgement, I'm going to teach you how to create/ co-create w/o boundaries. Whoever art project you're holding for the next song add to it. You're replacing the me w/ we.

Selfless: Now you're writing a love letter to your @ age 5. How proud of them you are, what they wouldn't believe you have accomplished & been through, How you're there for them, how amazingly epic they are ♡.

Playful: Beach Ball w/ Real Heart centered questions on it __BOOM__

12 - 10 - 19
Insanity is doing the same thing over and over again
and expecting different results.

Tapping into your Intuitive Bliss - The Act of giving selflessly - overview :

Who - heart centered individuals who want to connect to their Intuition

what - a 2 hour Art therapy class that focuses on the essentials of Intuition building

Why - to create ease & bliss when connecting to your magic. First 20 minutes will be an Introduction of everyone there. Then... Going over the basics of what Intuition really is: Your Intuition is your direct correlation to your dharmic Path. Your dharmic path, or dharma is the expression of your boundless, selfless creativity in alignment w/ the cosmic law - so basically what you are here for, your mission, your lifes work. It's everything that lights your soul on fire & fuels the world w/ compassion. it's when you replace the ME w/ WE, But how do we get into this headspace of selfless creation? We create to create, we create w/o judgement, w/o Boundaries, we see our creativity to the end of the project & not just stop halfway through. We create w/o expectation or the need for reciprication we create simply because it puts our mind at ease. Gratitude is the highest vibration of love & Love is non-judgemental, selfless, & playful, so when we learn to create from this place we can give from this place & when we give from this place we become a beacon or light to those still finding their way.

Practice the present.

I have everything I need.

It's easier to be human than to try to be God.

Faith is the opposite of fear.

Ask for help.

I am grateful for every moment
because time is so fleeting. I owe
this moment & every moment my
full presence. & it is an honor to
do so.

The only thing constant is change.

Lighten up.

Acceptance does not necessarily mean approval.

Success is getting what I want; happiness is wanting what I have.

Let go and let God.

Attitude of gratitude.

Detach with love.

I'd rather be happy than right.

First things first.

Frustration comes from lack of wisdom to know the difference.

The program in six words: Trust God, Clean House, Help Others.

I'm powerless over people, places, things and situations.

Make a decision then do it.

The difference between sobriety and serenity is surrender.

My perception of reality is a reflection of my inner self.

Keep it simple.

I'm given a road map but not a timetable.

- Listen to your gut when It says put your damn phone down

&

- Honor your Intuitive nudges

BOO! YOU GOT THIS!
Keep SHOWING UP!
Keep rising 2 The occassion!
Keep shining your beautiful light sister

I LOVE YOU! YOU GOT THIS!
its not about what they say or feel, its how you embody your gift + rise to the damn occassion every fucking day

The highest compliment is to listen.

Don't take it back—keep turning it over.

Humility means seeing things exactly as they are.

I'm not alone.

Anxiety is about the future; I can only deal with now.

I have to walk the walk—I can't just talk the talk.

Turn it over.

Give it up.

It feels good to feel good.

Thank God for what I've been given,
for what's been taken away, and for what's left.

Responsibility: Responding to my ability.

Go through the motions, the corresponding emotions will follow.

Recovery is a gift not a burden.

Our uniqueness makes us all the same.

God needs my help to make this a good day.

Surrender to win.

Success is never certain; failure is never final.

Change takes time.

Humility is not thinking less of me, but thinking more of you.

Wake up [6:30] - I have ALOT of FUN TO DO - TODAY
30 minute meditation / BATH / SHOWER

Bring Table in

Set scene
Create: 7 steps 2 CRE8
        SELFLESS SALES

Complete outline & RECORD
   · Course work
   · Notes etc.
   · Workbook

Certification : Reiki Master - Chakra Course
Send out Midweek motivation email.

30 minute yoga work

2 MILE RUN

USE FACE IN ALL EMAILS

Just for today.

12-11-19

It's not the elephants but the gnats that get me.

A coincidence is a miracle when God chooses to remain anonymous.

When I'm at the center of the universe, the universe is out of balance.

The only difference between a rut and a grave is in their dimensions.

Serenity is absence of fear, anger and guilt.

Seek results, not perfection.

Detachment is the wisdom to know the difference
between God's will and my will.

Success is just getting up again.

Live and let live.

Serenity is the acceptance of reality.

Work the Steps.

Isolation causes depression because there are no new experiences.

I can start over as many times as I need to.

HALT—don't get too hungry, angry, lonely or tired.

Fake it till I make it.

I don't have to handle it alone.

Easy does it.

If I want it to work, I have to work it.

I don't know what tomorrow holds, but I know Who holds tomorrow.

I'm not the one in control.

This means to me that their is something weighing really heavy on me. so heavy in fact that I feel lazy, tired, unmotivated, uninspired, depressed, afraid, my head feels super heavy, I cant get off my phone. I want results quicker than they're even possible, theres flipart of me that does not believe in myself whatsoever. I don't feel like I deserve friends, I dont know how to make friends, I'm afraid to really be seen by people, I'm anxious nervous, super underwhelmed, afraid to take aligned action daily

Daily aligned action :

- create IG Post
- GO LIVE ON TWITTER
- CREATE WORKSHOP FORMAT ✓
- FIND PLACE TO HOLD WORKSHOP ✓
- START ON 2nd Workbook + INCLUDE an E-COURSE
- CREATE E-course FORMAT

HOW 2 CRE8 a
FREEBIE THAT   a course in
SELLS - SELFLESS SALES

7 Steps 2 CRE8
SEIFRSS SALES

1. create something that has real value, what is real value
2. Freebies- why, How, who, what - your freebie should literally be priceless
3. Win- Win- Win structure
4. Why you're doing this: you're here to serve
5. What you're serving- cornerstones of your own healing / something that

When nothing's working, it's time for a meeting.

has worked for you, if you have nothing that has worked yet it's time 2 start creating

It doesn't matter what I think, what am I going to *do*?

Recovery is a process, not an event.

EGO: Easing God Out.

Either I am doing things to myself or I am doing things for myself.

Expectations create limitations.

By letting go of my wants, I get what I really need.

If it works, don't fix it.

Worry is a form of negative meditation.

The only thing worse than not getting my own way
is getting my own way.

It's not how I'm doing, it's how I'm trying.

Stay in today, stay out of the way.